HOW TO BE
SMART,
Successful,
&ORGANIZED
WITH YOUR **MONEY** ...

... FOR A BETTER **TODAY** AND **TOMORROW**!

Judith Heft

ISBN-13: 978-1536853742
ISBN-10: 1536853747

Editor: Dan Ruisi

Cover & Interior Design: Bryna Haynes, www.TheHeartofWriting.com

Cover photo credit: ProPhotos by Shannon

Printed in the United States.

ADVANCE *Praise*

"How you manage your money is a direct reflection of your beliefs about yourself. Getting better at managing your money is an act of self-worth. This indispensable manual shows you how to do just that by helping you get a handle on their daily financial flow. Read it. You're worth it."

- **FABIENNE FREDRICKSON**, founder of Boldheart.com

"Judy Heft is a rock star when it comes to helping people understand and manage their personal finances. This book covers it all, including how to deal with the least talked about, but most common, personal expenditures—such as what to do when you fall for the hard sell at your fitness club—the kinds of things so many of us are embarrassed to admit. Judy's writing is breezy, but direct, practical, and easy to understand. You'll find all the tools you need to live a life where you're in the financial driver's seat, building your own wealth instead of others'. Buy a copy for everyone you love. I am."

- **RUTH SHERMAN**, CEO & Celebrity Coach, Speaker, and author of *Speakrets*[R]: *The 30 Best, Most Effective, Most Overlooked Marketing and Personal Branding Essentials*

"Judy Heft shares countless ideas and suggestions in her well-constructed and thoughtful book. Within these pages there are more than mere morsels of best practices and warnings. She provides a down-to-earth approach to simplifying many aspects of everyday life that many find confusing. I recommend this book to anyone who feels overwhelmed or knows someone they wish to help get more organized about finances."

- ERIC A. KREUTER, PH.D., CPA, CGMA, CFE, Partner, Marks Paneth LLP, New York City/Westchester; Author of *Chasing Rainbows: An Existential Perspective of a Marathon Runner*

"Pragmatic ideas. Sharp insight. Honest recommendations. Just like when you are talking to Judy, her book speaks volumes from her experience and shows her value to her clients. Fun to read, this book is full of great material to be shared with others."

- MARC W. HALPERT, author of *LinkedIn Marketing Strategies for Law and Professional Practices: Techniques That Work*

"*How to Be Smart, Successful and Organized with Your Money* is an invaluable study, told in a straightforward manner that will appeal to everyone. Judy Heft's expertise in all fields of handling your finances is deftly told through this superb book. Fraud and especially Elder Abuse were two chapters that really hit home for me; the author provides us not only the 'warning signs' from these predators, but also divulges how you can prevent this from happening to yourself or your loved ones. So many other subjects are covered in this amazing volume. Ms. Heft really deserves praise for bringing this excellent publication to the forefront."

- LOU SABINI, Author of *They Were Expendable* and *Sex In the Cinema, the "Pre-Code" Years (1929-1934)*

"Judy Heft shares her considerable and sound knowledge and expertise guiding her clients with their finances and basics of daily living. It empowers the couple starting out and refreshes the family further along in life and career in making the right decisions, the smart decisions to stay whole. Basic common sense approaches. Follow the Judy."

- COREY BEARAK, ESQ., Author of *The Public Ought To Know*

"It is remarkable how little people know about the essentials of handling money, be it spending, saving, planning, reviewing, or budgeting. This book is awesome in that it speaks on every topic related to handling money for individuals and families. I found the section on Financial Literacy to be valuable, pointing out that small tricks of businesses can unsuspectingly cost you substantial dollars. Judy's warnings on consumer fraud, scamming, and abuse of elders is spot-on, and oh-so-critical for us all to be aware of. But the part I loved best is Chapter Eight, with its focus on the biggest financial regrets, such as this one: 'The biggest financial regret I made is that I put my children's private high school and university education at a higher priority than my own retirement.' Now *that* hits hard at home. Too often, we don't consider these things until after the fact, when it's too late. Judy makes sure you think of these things ahead of time. I needed this book thirty years ago!"

- HANS HANSON, author of *The Inside Secrets to Playing College Sports: What Every Mom and Dad Must Know!*

TABLE *of* CONTENTS

HOW TO BE

SMART,

Successful,

&ORGANIZED

WITH YOUR **MONEY**

CHAPTER *One*

A DAY IN THE LIFE

Woke up. Got out of bed. Worked out to clear my head.

That's how I begin every day. I find that it prepares me for whatever challenges are in store for me—and the average day brings plenty of challenges.

One day earlier this year, I kept a detailed journal of my activities, and I surprised even myself.

- **Processing the Mail:** I read the mail to a client who suffers from macular degeneration and took her bills back to my office where they would be paid, scanned, and shredded.

- **Daily Money Manager:** I stopped at another client's house to pick up her mail and have a brief meeting. We discussed the state of her accounts, and whether or not she needs funds transferred into the bill payment account to pay her estimated taxes and mortgage as well as other monthly expenses.

- **Interpreting a Letter From the New York State Government:** Being a Financial Concierge also means being an interpreter of government jargon. The next clients I helped had let go of their nanny, and subsequently received a notice from the New York State Department of Labor. According to the letter, their employer contribution rate to the unemployment office was increasing as a result of the firing. After explaining the situation to my clients, I provided them with an official New York State publication that explains the system.

- **Tracking Specific Expenses:** I was happy to see that one of my clients was keeping an eagle eye on his expenses when he contacted me for a report on landscaping expenditures. Because I categorize and track my clients' expenses, it took no time to print an easy-to-understand report.

- **College Tuition:** Another client needed me to verify that her child's college tuition had been paid and credited properly.

- **Internet Fraud:** A grandmother called me about some strange e-mails she had received. I helped her change her passwords on several accounts.

- **Elder Care:** I met with an elder care manager in order to find a new caregiver who was the right fit for a ninety-five-year-old client.

- **A Voice of Reason:** The daughter of a client got into a car accident, so I took care of the car accident report. I became concerned when my client's home health aide inserted himself into the picture, claiming to be qualified to do the body work on the damaged car. I explained to my client why this was a bad idea (lack of insurance, experience, etc.). She agreed to take the car to a professional.

- **Moving Logistics**: A couple I work for made the decision to downsize and move into a condo in a high rise building. It turned out that the air conditioning for the building was down, so we had to make other plans for them.

- **Shady Car Dealership:** A client was interested in buying a car, so he gave a dealership his American Express card to cover a deposit. When he decided not to buy the car, he discovered that the deposit had not been refunded. We contacted American Express and disputed the charge.

And no matter how busy I am, when my day is over, it's over. Barring any emergencies, after 6:00 p.m. is my time—and I hope you do the same for yourself. If you can't, then it may be time to hire a Financial Concierge to free up some of your valuable time.

CHAPTER *Two*
FINANCIAL LITERACY 101

Being American means being free, bold, and friendly ...

... Unless you've ever dropped a bunch of coins on the ground and dared not to pick up the pennies. People will give you dirty looks! And you know what they are thinking: "Oh, we have a big shot over here not picking up her pennies!"

It is in our nature to work hard and value every penny we have earned. We love deals and do amazing calculations in our brains when we're shopping. But what about saving money in the ordinary, mundane services that you already pay for?

CELL PHONE CARRIERS

Like cable companies (which we'll talk about later in this chapter), customer service representatives at wireless carriers hawk a long list of add-ons designed to balloon your bill to epic proportions. And the number-one offenders are unnecessary data subscriptions.

The last time I had the pleasure of spending hours in a wireless store, I was shocked to see how much data my salesperson had signed me up for, without even asking. Unless I got into the habit of watching YouTube videos all day at a location with no Wi-Fi, it is very difficult to imagine the scenario where I could possibly burn through 10 gigs of data in a month. Make sure to read your cell phone bill each time you receive it to monitor how much data you actually use—or get an app from the App Store or Google Play to do it for you.

CABLE PROVIDERS

Unlike cell phone carriers, cable providers are not generally inclined to negotiate prices. However, that does not mean you can't save some money. With the rise of "cord cutters," or people who rely solely on streaming services like Netflix, cable companies have become quite aggressive in pushing their bundle packages that include voice, data, and television plans. In fact, it is probably a good idea to review your bill to make sure they didn't "mistakenly" add any of those services.

It's an important point because packaged deals from the cable company do not always save you money. I know of one situation in which the "triple play" from a cable company cost more than paying for a separate phone line.

ELECTRICAL SUPPLIERS

In the 1990s, states began to "unbundle" electric service bills so there are now two separate charges:

- The energy supplier produces the energy. This is where you have a choice between a big utility company (like ConEd) or a smaller producer.
- The utility company (like ConEd) owns the power lines that deliver the energy.

Unfortunately, many people who chose to go with a smaller supplier are facing a price increase of 30 cents per kilowatt hour—and worse, many do not even know it. If I sound like a broken record, forgive me, but ... You should *always* read your bills in their entirety to see if you still need what you are paying for.

GYM MEMBERSHIPS

Going to the gym is great for the mind and body, but sitting down with a salesperson when you first join ... not so much. First they had me trying to consider the various joiner's fees against the various monthly charges. Next they started badgering me about personal trainers. The next thing I know they've got my belly fat in a caliper and I am signed up for personal training sessions every day at 6:00 a.m.

If this happens to you, don't worry. You can make it all go away as long as you cancel within three days, because there is a federal law that affords you that right.

BANK STATEMENTS

Banks make mistakes all the time. In my role as a Financial Concierge, I have seen banks make some serious, serious mistakes. The only way to guard against this is to know what you have, and the only way to do that is to balance your checkbook. Soon you will detect a bank error, and you will see how little things add up.

OTHER WAYS TO SAVE

- Auditing your insurance policies to make sure you are not insuring things that do not exist.
- Negotiating the price of heating oil.
- Reviewing your charges.
- Taking advantage of services that offer free shipping, like Amazon Prime.
- Paying attention to your monthly automatic debits.

It's easy to lose track of money when it's all a bunch of bleeps and bloops on a hard drive somewhere in California—but electronic money still spends the same, and I hope that one or more of these tips will help you recapture some of it!

The good news is that once a year you have the perfect opportunity to review your spending habits and devise a spending plan—"tax time."

The next time you find yourself gathering and tallying your tax documents at the kitchen table—of course with all the accoutrements like your accounting calculator, brass lamp with a green shade, and a stock ticker in the background—stop and really look at your receipts for the year for one hot minute. If you kept good records you would be able to see the various things you splurged on. You can take this knowledge and trim the fat this year.

Besides pleasing your accountant, detailed record-keeping also makes it easy to come up with the central theme of financial literacy: budgeting. And the overarching theme of your budget should be savings. An ample pool of cash standing by can mean the difference between surviving a life-changing event and persevering through it.

Another important point is that a spending plan is only as useful as the information you put in it (garbage in, garbage out). When you create a household budget, make sure to include your discretionary items, as well. Not only will they help you set limits, but they will help you establish goals.

Part of being financially literate is knowing when you are in over your head. And we would all be in over our heads if we tried to do our own taxes. I remember a friend telling me he was doing his own taxes…and he paid thousands more this year than he did with the help of an accountant the previous year, and his income had actually decreased.

Accountants are not the only financial professionals available to save you when you are in over your head. People like attorneys, Certified Divorce Financial Analysts, Certified Financial Planners, bookkeepers and daily money managers can be excellent resources—and, in the event your refund is dependent on some sort of writ or statement or schedule, they can be real lifesavers.

Not everybody is a detail-oriented paper person. Some

people are artists. (I am not—I can't even draw a stick figure!) If you always find yourself scrambling, trying to get things together and spending hours trying to understand what is tax deductible, it doesn't mean you are financially illiterate. The truly financially literate person recognizes that delegating tax preparation to an accountant is the opposite of penny wise and pound foolish.

Most people wouldn't dare attempt fixing plumbing problems without the help of a plumber. It is simply too important. The same is true when it comes to categorizing your expenses, preparing your will, or filing your taxes. The good news is that there are professionals available to look out for your interests.

A fiduciary is a person who holds a legal or ethical relationship of trust with one or more other parties (person or group of persons).

Certified Financial Planners (CFPs) are required to have fiduciary relationships with their clients. That means they are legally obligated to act in the best interest of the people who use their services. Another example of a fiduciary relationship is the relationship I have with my clients as a daily money manager.

Examples of how I act in the best interest of a typical client include:

- Reviewing bank accounts to ensure there are no errors.
- Paying close attention to insurance policies.
- Coordinating with family when necessary.
- Acting as a Power of Attorney when needed.

CFPs pick up where my expertise ends; they are most concerned with wealth planning. Since their area is inherently forward-looking, it often makes sense to involve younger generations in the planning process. **CFPs refer to this as generational planning, and it encompasses:**

- Looking at the whole picture over a number of years.

- Anticipating the future tax ramifications of family investments.

- Setting up different instruments like retirement accounts or donor-advised funds.

An important distinction to note is that, contrary to CFPs, stockbrokers are not fiduciaries.

A stockbroker's loyalty is not to the consumer, but rather to the company they work for. They are offered inducements to sell products according to their employer's priorities, not yours.

Such a large array of financial professionals may be hard to wrap your head around, so feel free to rely on this checklist:

- **Accountant:** Accountants spearhead the tax planning and strategy of a household.

- **Insurance Broker:** An independent broker (not an agent) can find the best policies from every insurer.

- **Certified Financial Planner:** These professionals are best able to assist with retirement planning and wealth preservation.

- **Attorney:** A qualified attorney (not an app or an online program) is best to draft wills, trust, estate plans, and other important documents.

- **Daily Money Manager:** A professional bookkeeper or daily money manager pays bills, categorizes expenses, organizes file systems, balances the checkbook, and acts as a liaison between the client and the rest of the financial team.

As you can see, there is ample help available to organize your finances and free up your time. I encourage you to consult with friends and family about their experiences and see if you can get some referrals to the professionals they use.

TALKING TO CHILDREN ABOUT MONEY

Whenever we talk to our young adult children about money, it's a good idea for us to be careful about what we say and how we say it.

For starters, don't come off as bossy or tell them what to do—because they may do the opposite just to spite us.

At the same time, adults learn a lot of lessons from our long, long histories of bad financial decisions, so it's only natural that we will want to share our wisdom with our children, especially if we are seeing them make basic financial mistakes, like:

- Lending money to friends
- Overspending

- Mixing business with pleasure
- Making bad credit decisions

Later on I will talk about how to communicate with your elderly parents, and I think some of the same rules apply. For instance, instead of telling them they are making a mistake, talk about a friend that you have who was once in a similar situation.

Another great strategy is to use "I" statements:

- I notice that you're very generous, and that's something I really love about you.

- I remember your father went into business with a friend, and it didn't end well.

- I'm so excited that you got your first credit card. You can increase your credit score if you pay it in full every month.

It is our responsibility to teach our kids how to be financially responsible adults, because it's hard for them to live on their own these days—unless you want them coming home after college!

CHAPTER *Three*

WHAT'S ACCOUNTING GOT TO DO WITH IT?

People use their business experience to inform their decisions in all areas of their lives, but none more so than running a household. And like any good business with a good bookkeeper, families benefit enormously from using accounting software.

Accounting software makes it easy to:

- Track your expenses in greater detail
- Record multiple streams of income
- Keep track of school and extracurricular expenses
- Manage your credit cards, debit cards and bank accounts

The most popular accounting programs for home use are Quicken and Mint. In addition to many other features, people fall in love with Quicken because it will never forget a transaction. For example, I worked with a family that was looking to hire a new landscaping company, and wanted to compare bids against what they spent last year. Using their accounting software, they pulled up all the relevant details they needed in order to make their comparisons.

Having all of your data ready to go as soon as tax season opens is perhaps the biggest reward for keeping your finances organized with software. Instead of panic or despair, you will be able to cheerfully comply when your accountant asks for figures on your:

- Charitable contributions
- Deductible medical expenses
- Property taxes
- Estimated tax payments
- Tax refunds
- Insurance premiums

Now is the perfect time to start.

After you meet with your accountant and estate attorney, your next move should be to meet with an insurance broker. I strongly encourage that everyone take a moment to think about long-term care insurance coverage—and how it works when life throws you a curve ball.

Grammar slam: If you are like me (surrounded by annoying grammar types), than u have asked urself many questies about insurance—especially whether insurance insures you are financially covered or if it ensures your are financially covered.

The answer is *ensures*. Insure is still a word, though. When an insurance company insures its policyholders, it ensures their policies are in effect.

The first thing you can do is to make sure you're with a good independent broker. **Many people do not know the difference between an insurance agent and an insurance broker, so I will break it down.**

- **Agent:** Works directly for one insurance company.
- **Independent Broker:** Sells insurance from more than one company.

If you're with an agency, verify that you're receiving the best rates possible. If you're with a broker, ask him or her to shop around for a better deal than you are currently getting.

Long-term care insurance is something that everybody, regardless of age or financial situation, should look into. It kicks in when the policyholder can no longer perform the six daily activities of life, which are:

- Eating
- Bathing
- Dressing
- Toileting
- Transferring (walking), and
- Continence

When choosing a long-term care policy, make sure to select one with an inflation or cost-of-living clause included, even if the premiums are higher. I have a client who chose a less-costly plan that did not include annual cost-of-living adjustments. While she is fortunate to have financial security, or any kind of long-term care insurance at all, I can easily see how her golden years would be a lot more comfortable if she had opted to pay a higher premium for better insurance.

Long-term care insurance and advanced directives may seem barely relevant to people who are young and vibrant ... or at least vibrant. But if you're getting married, having a baby, or going through any other life changes, there's no reason to leave it up to chance—and there's so much to lose if life catches you uncovered.

CHAPTER *Four*

YOUR LEGACY

Would you want Mom and Dad to be dealing with a rebellious teenager in their golden years? How do you want your property to be distributed? These are questions about your *legacy*.

APPOINTING A GUARDIAN

If your child is left with no living guardians and no one is assigned as such, your child's fate is at the mercy of the court. A judge will use the law to make his or her decision, often at the expense of common sense—like giving a boisterous toddler to your retired parents. Appointing a guardian ensures that your child lives with the people who are best able to care for him or her.

DIVIDING UP THE PROPERTY

Even if you don't have any children, you'll probably want a say over what happens to your property after you die. As an example, consider a person who owns a home and dies with no will in place, but several family members are seeking control of the estate. Probate court has jurisdiction over these matters.

A probate court (also called a surrogate court) is a specialized court that deals with matters of probate and the administration of estates, and the outcome of the proceedings of a probate court is rarely ideal.

REMEMBERING PEOPLE

Something that a probate court will never do is remember your housekeeper or your kind neighbor. Remembering people who are not in your family is not only a way to say "thank you," but it is also a sign that you have lived a rich life. If you want to remember certain people in your will, you should definitely include specific instructions.

While there are products and websites that offer templates for writing a will, a matter of this gravity deserves a professional trusts and estate attorney's expertise.

I was lucky growing up in the sense that my parents were transparent about where everything was located in the event that something happened to them. I am the same way with my children, and I encourage my clients to develop a similar transparency with their families.

CHAPTER *Five*

WHAT DID YOUR PARENTS TEACH YOU ABOUT MONEY?

If old adages are meant to offer guidance about the world, none ring truer than "Hindsight is 20/20." Unfortunately, unless we have a time machine, we are caught in a Catch-22 when we try to apply it. So why not listen to other people's hindsight instead?

That was my motivation when I reached out to my network and asked them "What did your parents teach you about money?" The responses were informative, inspiring, and well thought-out. Here are some of them.

My parents never spoke with me about money at all. It was a taboo and secret topic. On top of that, my mother was extremely financially irresponsible, spending way beyond her means and then just not paying her bills. Debt collectors were calling the house constantly. You can imagine without any other

*information or conversations with them the views I formed
about money! :) My absolute resolve to never turn out like my
mother is a large part of what drove me to succeed. I was never
going to turn out like her! (And didn't, thank God.) I wish
they had told me more, had open conversations, taught me how
to "balance" my checkbook, about investing, the stock market,
etc. I learned it all on my own.*

****

*My parents taught me early on that, whatever money I made,
I should save some of it. Over the years, you build a nest egg,
invest wisely, and diversify early, but you always will have
money and a foundation. Then your life's work will take you
from there and hopefully from those early lessons you learned
from your parents, it will carry through. I know because it's
worked for me and I'm sure many others as well.*

****

*I wish someone had strongly talked me into getting a prenup
and I wish I'd learned about budgeting and building an
emergency fund before setting out on my own. I also think
everyone needs a better understanding of what advisors they
need and how to hire them. (Thinking of CPAs, money
managers, financial planners, etc.)*

****

In general, the topic doesn't come up as much with women talking amongst women as it does with men talking amongst men. You know, men are taught to talk about the market with their buddies but women aren't. I really only have one girlfriend with whom we have shared a lot about our financial situations/ plans/ investments, etc.

****

My first thought is not to give in to the insanity around you as a young person buying a house or a middle-aged parent sending kids to college. Plenty of folks have done this before and gotten through it. Stay away from self-help books unless you first have a solid spiritual foundation yourself. Most of them simply add to panic. We have everything we need to make these decisions.

CHAPTER *Six*

GIVE ME SOME CREDIT

We all know that credit is the key to buying a home, taking fabulous vacations, and driving fantastic cars. At least for most of us.

Yet 40 million people have pretty serious mistakes on their credit report. In fact, one out of every five errors on people's credit reports adversely affect their credit scores. Credit reporting agencies have an obligation to fix these errors, but they don't.

So, what are some of their most common errors?

- Paid bills that are showing as delinquent
- Open accounts that are listed as closed
- Mistakes due to similar names and Social Security numbers

What makes the situation more difficult to navigate is the fact that the three credit reporting agencies (Experian, Equifax, and Transunion) have a dismal record of helping consumers out of their mistaken-identity nightmares. There is no number to call to speak to a customer service representative. A consumer who has done nothing wrong is drafted into a process that encourages people to quit in exasperation.

It starts with a lengthy online questionnaire which is unsatisfying and promises nothing, in addition to being emotionally draining.

A woman had a name mixup on her report and, as a result, she was not able to refinance her home, or get a car—or even sign her children's student loans. She even went so far as to contact her alleged creditors, who affirmed that she was not the debtor they were seeking. None of this mattered to the reporting agency. She ended up suing the credit reporting agency, and she won, but her justice was extremely delayed.

The takeaway is quite simple, and it's a familiar variation on a modern theme: **Credit rating agencies are not there to help consumers. They are around to make money, and the only way to do that is take the side of the creditors every time.**

Like everything, there is a time and place for using credit cards. They allow students to build up their credit scores, as long as they can steer clear of potential risks.

Anyone should be leery of anything offered as free, to pay later—especially impulsive college students who need school supplies, bubble gum and whatever else a college student would spend money on. But nothing is free.

For example, if Jane uses credit to buy something on sale and then doesn't pay the balance for two or three months, she ends up paying much more than the sale price of the item.

Here's how it goes.

- Jane pays sale price for the item.

- Jane thinks she's getting a bargain, but …

- Jane doesn't have the money to pay for it, so

- It's no bargain because Jane ends up paying interest and late fees on it.

Personally, I recommend using a debit card instead of a credit card. That is how a bright-eyed future doctor can live within his or her means. If they are smart and use their cards for emergencies only, they won't face the prospect of adding even more debt obligations on top of student loans.

60 percent of students borrow annually to cover tuition and fees. No one wants to graduate from college with extra debt—debt that is often largely composed of fees, "convenience charges"—and, of course, interest.

Interest for credit cards is usually expressed as APR. APR stands for Annual Percentage Rate, and is simply the finance charge for a loan or credit card expressed as an annual rate. The true APR of a credit card is often masked by introductory interest rates, so anyone applying for credit should read the fine print. A missed payment may lead to double or triple the interest rate— just for being late. Even if it is by one day, interest rates can go as high as 29 percent.

Talk to your college student about interest and the penalties of defaulting on credit card debt. And whatever you do, don't co-sign credit cards—save your ability to co-sign for the fun world of student loans!

CHAPTER *Seven*

THE MOST PATRIOTIC THING YOU CAN DO: YOUR TAXES

Let's talk about taxes. As the days start getting shorter and your accountant savors the last few months of peace before the end-of-year rush revs into gear, why not make his or her job easier?

I've put together a list of some of the things you should be thinking about before year end. Being prepared might just save you some money!

CHARITABLE CONTRIBUTIONS

- If you have contributed over $250 to any one organization, make sure you have the acknowledgement letters that you received.

- Make sure your charitable contributions are sent out by December 1, because the IRS looks at the date the check was cashed, not the postmark, when examining your contributions.
- In-kind donations are valued at the fair market price. For example, an old car donated to a charitable cause would be valued at the resale price.

CREDIT REPORT

- The three credit reporting agencies are each required to issue a free credit report once a year to consumers.
- If you haven't checked already, I strongly encourage looking up your credit score every four months to take advantage of the free reports – or at the very least, once a year. You can find them at www.AnnualCreditReport.com.

ESTATE PLANNING

- The end of the year is a good time to review your will. Any changes to your will take effect immediately.
- If you have a trust in place naming a beneficiary, it will supersede your will.

HEALTH SAVINGS ACCOUNTS (HSAS) AND FLEXIBLE SPENDING ACCOUNTS (FSAS)

There are important differences between these two types of pre-tax accounts:

- FSAs are accounts that are owned by your employer. You must spend all the money in an FSA by the end of the year or you will forfeit it.
- HSAs are accounts owned by the holder (you). With an HSA, if there is money left over from this year, it will be rolled over into next year.

PRESERVING WEALTH

- Starting in 2013, the annual gift tax exclusion increased to $14,000 for an individual and $28,000 for a couple.
- If you have set up life insurance or an irrevocable life insurance trust for someone, premiums paid on these policies are considered gifts and count against the annual gift tax exemption of $14,000 per individual.
- Another way to avoid taxes is to pay for an individual's medical or educational expenses – but only if you pay the institution directly. There is no tax on this sort of giving.

RETIREMENT ACCOUNTS

If you surpassed seventy-and-one-half years old, you have to take your required minimum distribution from your IRA accounts.

Any distributions from a retirement account are considered taxable income.

Planning early for taxes is your best chance at maximizing your tax savings—not only because of your deductions and credits, but also because your accountant will only need to do a fraction of the work he or she normally does for clients.

Your accountant will be able to assess your fiscal situation and advise you on things such as your retirement plan, charitable contributions, and other deductions that might lower your tax bill.

Before you meet with your accountant, here are some other things you should have ready:

- Property tax bills for the year.
- Letters from the charitable organizations you donated to—a letter should detail the monetary value of your gift to the organization.
- Relevant reports from Quicken or QuickBooks— and make sure the entered data is accurate and up to date.
- If you hand-write your checks, make sure you have all your receipts and that they are detailed enough to categorize the expense.
- Medical deductions for the year, if you qualify.

People with IRAs and 401Ks should make sure they have maxed out their contributions for the year, including catch-up contributions. The maximum contribution for individuals under fifty is $5,500 per year, while people over fifty are allowed to contribute $6,000. It's best to see an accountant to ascertain your particular situation, because the laws governing retirement accounts can get rather complex in certain instances. If newly self-employed, make sure to open a self-employed retirement (SEP) account.

FLEX ACCOUNTS

Flexible Spending Accounts (FSAs) allow you to buy health-related products with pre-tax dollars. The program is very popular but requires a taxpayer to "use it or lose it," meaning that funds left in your Flex account will be forfeited at the end of the year.

While it is possible to obtain a refund, the money disbursed back to you will once again become subject to taxes. To take advantage of the tax savings this program was designed to offer, it's best to "use it." Most items in a drugstore are eligible for flex spending.

BONUSES AND GIFTS

The end of the year is also the time of year when employers show their appreciation to their employees by issuing bonuses. All bonuses or gifts from an employer to an employee must be taxed, whether it's an extra week's pay or a smaller lump sum.

The exception is if your workers are actually employed by a third party, like an agency or temp service. In those cases your gift or bonus would be considered a gift between two private individuals.

FREQUENT FLYER AND CREDIT CARD REWARDS

Not only can they be used for flights or upgrades, they are increasingly being used as negotiating tools. But are they really worth all the trouble?

People often ask me if frequent flyer miles are taxable, and the answer is no. According to the IRS, it "...has not pursued a tax enforcement program with respect to promotional benefits such as frequent flyer miles."

Using airline miles and credit card rewards to help pay for a business expense, however, will reduce the cost basis of the goods being purchased.

For example, let's say that:

- You buy a $499 laser printer for your business.
- Luckily, you can save $50 by using your credit card rewards points.
- You are then only allowed to deduct the balance of $449 as a business expense.

Some people just don't "get" rewards programs—and I get that. They point to the fact that flights are cheap and that the rewards come with so many conditions that they are, more often than not, unusable. Personally, I hoard my miles because I feel like I would be wasting them—I'm always saving them for "something better."

CHAPTER *Eight*

WHAT IS YOUR BIGGEST FINANCIAL REGRET?

You can learn from your mistakes. Hindsight is 20/20. History forgotten is history repeated.

These may be clichés, but there is more than an ounce of truth to them. That's why I decided to reach out to my friends and colleagues and ask the question, "What is your biggest financial regret?"

My friends being as awesome as they are, the answers I got were not only interesting but thoughtful. And as our first commenter notes, there is a common theme:

> *The two things that I see almost every client experiencing are that they did not start saving early enough towards retirement, or toward financing the education of their children. The result is, in many cases, having to cut back on lifestyle to finance these two goals. The alternative in the education financing often is burdening their children with exorbitant student loans.*

Next up is someone who works in the financial industry with some of their own inside information:

> *The biggest financial regret I made is that I put my children's private high school and university education at a higher priority than my own retirement.*
>
> *Today, as a professional comprehensive financial planner, I sometimes counsel my clients differently.*
>
> *Of course, it's unique to each client, but some clients should save into your tax-deferred accounts first because those funds aren't counted in the university's scholarship and grant pool. And today, there are so many more opportunities for the children to qualify for grant and scholarship money—and are often need-based.*
>
> *If the child needs to take out subsidized Stafford loans in junior or senior years (interest starts six months after graduation) the parents' funds continue to grow in the interim and when the parents turn fifty-nine-and-a-half they can withdraw funds to cover the children's shortfall—if there is one. Depending on where the child begins his career, there are also many more sign-on bonuses where a company will cover the child's student loans once he/she is hired.*

Retirement surfaces again in this next testimonial, but it also brings up the issue of "staying home with the kids":

> *Here are my biggest regrets:*
>
> *1) Not scraping together the money when I was twenty-six years old to buy a town home in Hoboken. I could see that it was just ready to emerge and since then real estate has done very well there.*

2) Although I have saved more than most people my age for retirement, as I approach fifty (I just turned forty-eight), retirement and the amount of money needed for that seems "right around the corner," and I am worried about my ability to save enough to live as comfortably as I want. I wish that I had saved more, earlier. Especially because this would have not been a huge impact on my overall lifestyle yet would have meant the difference between buying five new shirts that month or one. Even that small amount would have added up to a lot so that now it would not feel so daunting! I know I'll make it there but wish I was further along.

3) I took a year and a half off when [my son] was born, and another two and a half years [after that]. Although I know I did the right thing for him by being around more, it was a big financial impact and I lost four years of income in my highest earning years. So although I don't know if I ultimately would have done anything differently, I do sometimes lament that I could have been a lot further along now in securing financial security.

Some comments were as humorous as they were insightful:

That I did not get long-term care insurance when I was young enough to make it affordable.

******

I didn't start a retirement savings plan early in my career.

****

That my husband is also a self-employed person!

And lastly, the single, solitary bits of wisdom that didn't mention retirement:

Purchasing a timeshare with my partner that we never use and cannot sell!

****

Breaking the lease for our office space and being taken to court, with the result being tens of thousands of dollars in rental fees paid out of pocket!

CHAPTER *Nine*

CHARITABLE GIVING

Charitable giving occupies an important place on your moral compass. You want to give to the dozens of great organizations vying for your donation, but you know it's impossible.

Here are a few things to remember when navigating the sea of end-of-year solicitations that deluge your mailbox:

- **Check to make sure you haven't donated to them already this year.** (This goes back to the untold, hidden joys of good record keeping.) I was with a client recently who was overwhelmed by donation requests, and feeling guilty for not giving more. I first explained that someone who is on a fixed income should be granted a little slack.

Second, I told her that she had already given to
several of the charities that were now asking for a
year end donation—and that she could expect to
receive dozens more requests from each charity.

- **Beware of charities that try to make themselves
  look like heavy hitters who have been operating
  for years.** Very often their names are slight
  variations of legitimate charities, and this might
  be enough to fool someone with limited eyesight,
  for instance. This is especially true after a disaster
  happens: Up to 60 percent of the 4,000 charity
  websites that emerged in the wake of Hurricane
  Katrina were found to be phony.

- **Reputable charities spend at least 75 percent
  of their donations on programs and services.**
  Be wary of any organization that claims to use less
  than 75 percent of their revenue on programs and
  services.

- **If you give over $250 to an entity and wish to
  use it as a deduction, you must obtain a letter
  of confirmation from the organization(s).** In
  some cases, like when donating to a thrift store,
  you will be given a generic receipt to fill out
  yourself. Most charities are diligent about providing
  proof of your donation, but again, good record
  keeping is the key to ensuring you get the same tax
  credit as everyone else did for their generosity.

- **Never give to a charity that solicits your donation over the phone.** Giving out a credit card number over the phone is a disaster waiting to happen for a variety of reasons, including complicated scams as well as such mundane dangers as someone eavesdropping.

DONOR-ADVISED FUNDS

Donor-advised funds (DAF) provide immediate tax-savings and are excellent for people who are unsure of where to spend their charity dollars.

A DAF is a philanthropic vehicle that allows donors to make charitable contributions and receive immediate tax benefits—as opposed to going through all the aggravation and expense of having a family foundation. According to Wikipedia:

To participate in a donor-advised fund, a donating individual or organization opens an account in the fund and deposits cash, securities, or other financial instruments. They surrender ownership of anything they put in the fund, but retain control over how their account is invested, and how it distributes money to charities.

In addition to the immediate tax benefits, a DAF is versatile in the kinds of donations it can accept, which include:

- Cash donations
- Securities
- Jewelry

- Artwork
- Bereavement gifts that were made in lieu of flowers

One important limitation of DAFs is that disbursement can only be made to 501(c)(3)-designated charities. It is also possible, but unlikely, that the DAF may refuse to honor the wishes of the donor.

But with the overhead costs of family foundations reaching upwards of 4 percent of their endowments, DAFs are becoming more and more attractive to high-net-worth families who:

- Have selected a favorite 501(c)(3) target charity
- Wish to make charitable contributions that can be deducted for the current year
- Have no taste or inclination for chasing after charities for proof of donations

EDUCATING YOUR KIDS ABOUT CHARITABLE GIVING

Charitable giving can also be a powerful tool to give your kids an education about the value of a dollar. Consider giving them some seed money for them to start their own philanthropic mission.

Let them identify a few charities they like and watch as they figure out a budget. They may not know they are making a budget, but when they have a fixed amount of money to spread around three or four different charities, that is exactly what they are doing. Will they choose to give an equal amount to every one of their causes, or will they see that by making a larger gift they can make a bigger impact?

Of course not all charitable contributions—and not all lessons about the value of a dollar—have to be made with cash, check or credit card. Time is money. The gift of time is something that my family and I love to donate each summer to a pretty special place called Camp Happy Times.

Sponsored by the Valerie Fund, this week-long respite for kids who have or have had cancer does not seem like work because it is so much fun.

The program requires that once the campers graduate from high school, they also graduate camp. Though always welcome, they are not eligible to return and participate as Leaders in Training until they take a year off to mature a little. A transformation occurs during this summer off; these young people have lived as adults and they know the value of a dollar. Even so, they are eager to volunteer a week of their valuable time.

And while charitable giving is something that makes our country and our society stronger, let's not lose sight of the goal of parenting; when you teach your kids fiscal responsibility, you are giving them an advantage in life. It's like giving them the gift of a car, graduate school, and a house all at the same time.

CHAPTER *Ten*

CREATING A SPENDING PLAN

As I've already established, time is merciless in its march into the future. The swath of destruction it leaves is even visible on our faces.

In addition to filling our gyms beyond capacity on January 2, many of us choose to tone up our wallets, usually in the form of a do-or-die budget. But budgeting does not need to be perfect. In fact, the people who allow themselves greater flexibility with their spending plans are the ones who have the best chance of success.

Here are some ways to succeed with your spending plan:

- **Create Monthly Spending Plans:** Many people abandon their budgets because sticking to them seems overwhelming. I have found that the people who get overwhelmed are planning year to year.

Instead, my advice is to budget month to month in order to maintain a better grasp of what you are spending.

- **K.I.S.S.** When creating a spending plan for the new year, keep it simple. Creating a plan that is overly detailed makes it much more likely to become an abstract concept rather than something practical.

- **Allow the Easy Fixes:** When tracking your progress in adhering to your spending plan, remember that being flexible also allows you to adjust, completely change, or delete aspects that have shown themselves to be unrealistic—the biggest threat to any spending plan is having items that you continually ignore or forget about.

- **Take Baby Steps:** Let's be honest: No one really wants to spend less money, just like no one really wants to cut the lawn. A friend of mine was recently telling me how he made lowering his expenditures easier, just by changing his mindset. He said that just the idea of saving money influenced the way he spends, and according to him, it was effortless. In other words, he took baby steps toward accomplishing his goal, and it had a real impact. Never underestimate the power of baby steps!

- **Take Advantage of Your Credit Card(s):** Credit cards are great for emergency expenses, and many offer detailed reporting as well. For example, Discover includes your credit rating with every statement—without negatively affecting your credit.

- **Use Cash:** Yes, cash still exists, and yes, stores still accept it. One piece of advice I give to people who are trying to rein in their holiday spending is to make an envelope with each person's name on it, and stuff it full of cash…but only the cash you want to spend. Then you can leave your credit cards at home and be proud of your restraint.

The takeaway is simply to be realistic. Make sure your spending plan reflects your lifestyle, cut yourself some slack, and take a long-term view of your finances. Do your budgeting in a way that is suited to your personality and capabilities—and know that falling off your horse and getting back on it is a time-honored tradition shared by most successful people!

CHAPTER *Eleven*

RECORD KEEPING BEFORE AND DURING DIVORCE

From experience, I have learned that many people pay their bills without performing any serious record keeping.

This can become problematic if there is ever a divorce, especially when compounded with the emotional trauma that comes with divorce.

In Connecticut, divorcing parties must provide the court with a Financial Affidavit. In New York, a corresponding form is used, called a Statement of Net Worth. Both are court documents, which must be filled out accurately under the penalty of perjury.

Helping people with the required documentation they need to show for their divorce has been a core part of my business for over fifteen years and, let me tell you, guesstimating doesn't cut it! The forms ask exactly what a person's weekly expenses are on a very detailed level for each family member.

The information needed for divorce forms includes, but is not limited to:

- Mortgage payments
- Medical expenses
- Education
- Car expenses
- Clothing
- Entertainment
- Maintenance of the house

It's important to note that the end-of-year reports some credit card companies send out, which break down the charges into spending categories, are not very accurate and will not be sufficient for a divorce affidavit. The categories the credit card companies use are typically very vague and often they do not even get that right.

I once had a client whose haphazard record keeping almost resulted in an epic accounting disaster for her. She was referred to me by her divorce attorney to help with her financial affidavit. She didn't have any understanding of the cash flow for the house and she had never written any checks to pay any of the household bills. When her divorce was finalized, she was awarded alimony, but as the years went on her husband's earning potential changed. As a result, she had to keep going back to court for reevaluations of the alimony plan, which meant she had to keep filling out financial affidavit after financial affidavit. Luckily for her, I had her back each time.

I think a lot of people are just like my client, not really knowing in any kind of detail how they spend their money. Most people are happy to remember to pay their bills on time. That's great, but that's not the same as keeping good books; that's just paying your bills on time. Getting it all organized in a program such as Quicken or Quickbooks and getting all the little details correct is important, not just for financial affidavits, but for tax reporting purposes as well.

While the benefits of keeping good records may not be immediately apparent, the odds are that, with time, it will pay off. Of course no one ever starts out with a plan to divorce, or to get audited by the IRS—but life happens. You never know what the future might bring.

CHAPTER *Twelve*

WELCOME TO THE FUTURE

The internet is older than most of your coworkers, your car has more intelligence than you do, and your phone is capable of interstellar travel. So what are you doing writing out your budgets and expenses with pen and paper?

THE MERITS OF ACCOUNTING SOFTWARE

With accounting software, you can:

- Track your expenses in greater detail
- Record multiple streams of income
- Keep track of school and extracurricular expenses
- Manage your credit cards, debit cards, and bank accounts

As I've mentioned before, the most popular accounting software for home use is Quicken. In addition to many other features, people fall in love with Quicken because it will never forget a transaction.

For example:

A family is looking to hire a new oil delivery company, and they want to compare bids against what they spent last year. Using their accounting software, they pulled up all the relevant details they needed in order to make their comparisons.

Having all of your data ready to go as soon as tax season opens is perhaps the biggest reward for keeping your finances organized with software. Instead of panic or despair, you will be able to cheerfully comply when your accountant asks for figures on your:

- Charitable contributions
- Deductible medical expenses
- Property taxes
- Estimated tax payments
- Tax refunds
- Insurance premiums

Now is the perfect time to "get with it"—so what are you waiting for?

FEAR OF MISSING OUT—
AKA, OVERSHARING

TMI. Airing your dirty laundry. Oversharing. These are all things that existed before the internet, and while they made for entertaining gossip in 1995, today they have become too commonplace to really enjoy—and their consequences too dire.

Social scientists have researched this phenomenon and applied an old theory to it called Fear of Missing Out.

Fear of missing out, or FoMO, is "a pervasive apprehension that others might be having rewarding experiences from which one is absent." This social angst is characterized by "a desire to stay continually connected with what others are doing."

The following are just a few of the negative consequences of sharing every aspect of your life on social media.

IDENTITY THEFT

There is a treasure of information located on the vast array of social media servers in Silicon Valley and beyond. This triad of personal information is available to anyone on Facebook, by default:

- **Name:** Your name is the first step to taking over your identity.

- **Date of Birth:** This is an important step under the medical privacy law HIPAA to authenticate your identity.

- **Address:** This can be obtained by looking at pictures that have been geotagged.

Right there is enough information for a bad guy to show up at your pharmacy and pick up your medications. Privacy experts encourage social media users to "tweak" their displayed names or use a nickname (even though it is against the rules on Facebook). Also consider not making your date of birth visible or using a fake birthday. Lastly, for all that is dear, stop geotagging your pictures!

DIVORCE

Even with innovative new methods like mediation and collaborative divorce, breaking up is hard to do. Judges in New York have allowed private posts to be submitted into evidence in divorce proceedings, and have ruled that tagging an ex-spouse in unflattering pictures can be deemed harassment in some cases. Beyond tagging, consider these real examples:

- Geotagging can be used to prove any number of things, such as infidelity and dissipation of marital funds.

- Friends tagging you in pictures at parties that show you consuming alcohol or worse (like when you are geotagged in Colorado) can do you a great disservice at child custody hearings.

- Plain old text posts that appear vindictive or mention seemingly innocuous details about the status of your divorce can create bad blood and force you into a much more costly proceeding.

You can un-tag your own pictures and keep yourself from writing posts with TMI, but how can you stop your friends and acquaintances from tagging you in a picture where you are doing a keg stand? On Facebook you have the option of disallowing other people from tagging you without your permission. Believe me, it's a good thing.

WON'T SOMEBODY THINK OF THE CHILDREN?

I am lucky enough to be a nana twice over, with each of my two daughters becoming a mother in the last three years. Both of my daughters are on Facebook, and each has her own preferences for sharing pictures of my little grandbabies; one shares pictures prudently and the other shares practically none.

Do I wish they'd each share more? Sometimes. But I also know they are being smart, probably smarter than me—there have been cases of kids' identities being stolen, completely unknown to the kids and parents until the kids reach the age of majority and see that they have negative credit.

Facebook privacy settings can be adjusted to suit your needs and personality, but remember: Facebook is a money-making machine, and the things you post will always be analyzed by someone or something.

CHAPTER *Thirteen*

DO YOU WANT YOUR ONLINE PROFILES DELETED AFTER YOU DIE?

W here will your family go to remember you after you die? **Hint: The answer is not a graveyard.**

I sometimes wonder what would happen if I abandoned my social media presence. Well, I got my answer the other day when LinkedIn managed to make me feel awkward in my own office. Several of my connections have died over the years, so it was a little uncomfortable when I saw one of them was celebrating a work anniversary.

Oh no, I thought, *now it's like he's the butt of a joke.*

So I decided to query my friends about the issue of memorializing or deleting social media accounts. The majority of those polled wish to have their Facebook profiles deleted, however there were some people who preferred to memorialize their timelines.

Here are some of the things they said:

I have a few friends that have passed away. People still comment on their Facebook pages. It's kind of nice to see and read comments people have left as a memorial! It's kind of like a digital headstone!

****

Deleted please. Something to think about. I should probably let them know...

****

Well, since you asked, I want my Facebook account to be memorialized and beamed into outer space so that all of creation can know about this comment.

****

I deleted a friend yesterday who had passed away some time ago. It was weird, but I did enjoy seeing his smiling face & photos!

****

This is a good but creepy point. I guess I'd rather have my friend there than not but I can't put words around it.

The issue of ghost accounts is not just one of pride; your personal identifying information will still be found in a variety of places online, including:

- Real and junk e-mail accounts alike.

- Photos on Facebook or Instagram.

- Resumes posted on LinkedIn.

- Music and documents stored in the Cloud.

- Online banking records and accounts.

- Frequent flier accounts.

Creating a digital will allows people to prevent that sort of thing from happening. A digital will appoints a digital executor who will "execute" your wishes and directives.

Choosing a digital executor should be done with caution. They should be capable, tech savvy, and above all, trustworthy: You will be entrusting him or her with all of your passwords. Your online executor is powerless without your passwords. But what if you change your passwords every month like I do?

PC Magazine recently published a guide to password managers that I found extremely useful. The range of different features that each product offers is a lot to take in, so I will spare you the time and say Last Pass looks the best on paper.

Some websites have taken it upon themselves to develop easy-to-use "legacy" programs of their own, but none more so than Facebook. A new feature, one that I hope to never use, allows any friend or family member to request that a deceased person's timeline be turned into a memorial. Proof is required, usually in the form of an obituary.

LinkedIn has a similar process for removing the profiles of deceased members.

Other, specialized websites serve as eternal obituaries, promising to keep your loved one's memory alive forever—or at least until the sun consumes the earth in five billion years

Personally, I don't want my online presence to continue after I die. I just want to be remembered as a good mom and nana, and a kind and generous person.

CHAPTER *Fourteen*

GETTING ORGANIZED

I t happens: bills go unpaid.

People may neglect their bills for a variety of reasons, like depression or exhaustion. Many people have a "system" that often consists of nothing more than plastic bags filled with unopened mail and shut-off notices from utility companies. But sometimes there is hidden gold in those piles of paper.

In one such case, almost as an afterthought, a client alerted me to the fact that she uncovered several more bags worth of mail for me to go through. In doing so, I discovered a check for $16,000 that probably would have been thrown out if I had not gone through each piece of mail, leaving no stone unturned.

At another client's house, I found myself looking over her car insurance policy, and scratching my head. The premium was for the coverage of five automobiles, yet I knew I had never seen that many cars in the driveway of the house. I confirmed this with my client and it turned out she was paying insurance for a non-existent car. The insurance agent had been sloppy and allowed this to go on. I contacted them and ultimately got a refund for my client.

So, if you feel overwhelmed by the sheer volume of bills coming to your house every month, resist the temptation to crawl into bed and hide under the sheets until they go away. **If you can't do it all yourself, get help.**

I always cringe when a TV show or a movie has a plot twist where one of the characters is wandering alone somewhere, just a few feet away from help, but she never realizes it and ends up having some sort of a bad thing happen to her.

I feel the same frustration when I hear people say things like "But I can't get organized!" Yes, you *can* get organized, help is just around the corner! And if you are the DIY type, there is still help available, like these **5 Secrets to Organization:**

- **Sweep Your Desk, Office, or Kitchen Counter On a Regular Basis**: It doesn't have to be every day, but it does have to be consistent. An unexpected bonus to having a clean work space is increased concentration!

- **Open Your Mail Daily:** Touch it once, act on it, and get it out of your sight. Forever.

- **Get a Sturdy, Cross-cut Shredder:** Hover over it while you are sorting the mail, so that it is actually physically easier to dispose of the junk.

- **Adopt the 90-10 Rule:** As you are sorting, throw away 90 percent, and only keep 10 percent. If you are unsure of whether or not to keep something, ask yourself:

  - Do I need it?

  - Is it important, as a memory?

  - What are the reasons I'm keeping it?

  - Does the next generation really care?

- **Check Your Credit Report Once a Year:** We are entitled to one free credit report from each credit reporting agency every year. If there are mistakes, it is best to take care of them sooner rather than later.

As they say, "A rolling stone gathers no moss." I don't know who "they" are, but they've got a point. Staying on top of your filing is the only way to avoid miserable nights during tax season. The good news is your file system can be tailored to your personality, and keeping up with it can be effortless.

My mother was extremely organized, and it always looked effortless. Naturally, I was a rebellious kid who embraced disorganization ... and I became an adult who married disorganization, figuratively and literally.

Together, my Was-Band (He WAS my husBAND) and I each managed our own businesses quite well down in the valleys of mountains of unopened mail. When we split up, I moved out of the "house that clutter built" and decided to take very little with me to my new place.

All of a sudden, I was enjoying the roominess of a new, uncluttered home. Where once my previous dining room had been converted into my home office, I now had a dining room I could dine in—and it was delicious.

Getting started is surprisingly easy, and costs nothing, with these baby steps into the world of efficiency:

- **Throw Out Your Junk Mail:** You need to be merciless when freeing yourself from this unsolicited nuisance. That's why I recommend opening your mail while standing over a shredder.

- **Keep a Clean Desk:** I know first hand that keeping a clean desk allows you to get things done faster and better—which is why I have always subscribed to the old adage: "A cluttered desk is a sign of a cluttered mind."

- **File it, Keep it, Toss it:** When a new piece of paper comes into your office, you should deal with it immediately—whether you file, keep or toss it.

- **Use Online Statements:** In our offices we do not retain bank statements or credit card statements because they are available online. In fact, we have been paperless since 2013.

- **Trash It:** Holding onto things you don't need is how clutter thrives and reproduces. Don't be afraid to throw out unneeded or unwanted things.

Most people come to organizers with quite a backlog of information that needs to be sifted through. It can be quite daunting, but it is possible to get it all done if you set aside a modest amount of time every day to do it. And remember that when you hire a professional organizer, you're really forming a partnership. Both parties have responsibilities, but the goal is to make them as quick and painless as possible for you.

Side-stepping the printer and using accounting software such as Quicken to interface directly with the banks conserves things I know my grandchildren will need in the future, like trees.

Some vendors do not have the ability to set up online invoicing and others are required by law to use paper invoicing. Even if a paper invoice is unavoidable, digitizing it is a good idea.

The latest generation of document scanners can process twenty-five pages per minute, front and back. Some scanners are set up to work with any size or type of paper, including register receipts and business cards. Because of the way smart scanners recognize text and can produce editable and searchable documents, it makes sense for me to scan things even if I am required to retain the hard copy.

As a professional financial organizer and daily money manager, I know what happens when people take on too much change at once. Meltdowns happen. That is why I took baby steps on my journey to achieve my latest goal: Becoming paperless.

Though it was frustrating at first, I stuck to my guns and did the right thing.

If you are also considering making the switch, you might find yourself feeling very uneasy throwing certain documents into the shredder. The following is a brief list of some documents, and whether you should run them through the scanner or shredder:

- **Bank Statements:** These are not necessary to archive since most banks allow you to download statements for up to seven years.

- **Brokerage Statements:** These should be kept until you sell the securities.

- **Capital expenses:** Keep the invoice for any major purchases for your home or your condo for as long as you own the property, for depreciation purposes.

- **Charity Appreciation Letters:** Charities thank donors with typed out, old-fashioned letters of appreciation. Keep these together with the tax returns for the corresponding year.

- **Credit Card Statements:** These do not need to be retained unless there is a charitable contribution included or if you have medical expenses that you itemize on your taxes.

- **Insurance Policies:** These can be discarded when a new one is issued.

- **Legal documents:** Birth certificate, marriage license, divorce decree, will, living wills, etc. should be kept permanently in a safety deposit box or other safe place.

- **Pay Stubs:** These should be retained for a year or until you receive your 1099 or W2.

- **Phone and Utility Bills:** These are not necessary to keep unless they are for your business.

- **Retirement accounts:** Keep your IRA, SEP, and 401K contributions permanently.

- **Purchase Invoices and Receipts:** Small businesses should keep a log of their purchases and archive that along with the tax return of the corresponding year.

- **Vendors' Monthly Statements:** These do not need to be retained.

A good rule of thumb is that if an item appears on your tax return, you should hold on to the receipt for seven years.

CREATING A SYSTEM

One of the most overlooked aspects of running a business is to create a system. **You need a system. I need a system. Everybody needs a system.**

I'm not talking about your circulatory system, or your nervous system—indeed, the system I am talking about will make you a *lot* less nervous.

Creating a system is not unlike a part of mathematics called algorithms. An algorithm is a step-by-step instruction manual for any given task. In this context the task is not so much having a week of stellar sales figures, but having a week on the shores of the Caribbean Sea in the middle of January; by having a well defined set of instructions, it will be easier to leave your work at work, and, occasionally, leave frigid climates for warmer ones.

The most daunting part of creating a system is not really that daunting at all. It simply requires that you take an inventory of all the things you do at your job, including the rote, almost mechanical functions that you perform without thinking about them. Just because you don't think about it does not mean it is unimportant. It makes the difference between your business running smoothly and having to sift through piles of post-its with basic questions scrawled all over them when you return from the Caribbean.

Having a systems binder in place also makes the process of on-boarding new hires much easier. If it is comprehensive enough, it can be used to answer any questions a new employee might have about how to handle different tasks, situations, and clients.

And systems are not set in stone; they should be constantly evolving and adjusting to reflect new experiences that you have learned from. For example, I was at a Mastermind meeting a couple of weeks ago when a speaker was set to address the crowd in heels …on a hardwood floor. She decided to send an assistant to get a rug to stand on, making the speech she gave more about the things she was saying than the clap of her hard shoes against the hard floor. As a result of this experience, her systems manual now includes the task of checking whether or not the venue has a hard floor—and her trunk now includes a carpet in case it does.

Specific items that should be a part of any system, whether business or personal, should include:

- How does the mail get processed?
- How are voice-mails recorded and replied to?
- Where do bills go?
- How do you pay vendors?

Each system I create is customized to suit the client's individual needs. They can trust that we'll do what we say we're going to do, and that we'll follow up.

If you're thinking about creating a system for your business or personal life, start by writing a rough draft that you are not committed to. For ideas on how to do this, check out the book *Work the System* by Sam Carpenter.* Alternatively, professional organizers are available to help you articulate your system, put it in place, and grow your business.

CHAPTER *Fifteen*

CUTTING THROUGH THE JARGON: WHAT "BEST PRACTICES" ACTUALLY LOOK LIKE

W hat is a "Best Practice?

Best Practice: A method or technique that has consistently shown results superior to those achieved with other means, and that is used as a benchmark. In addition, a "best" practice can evolve to become better as improvements are discovered.*

Being a bookkeeper, organizer and Financial Concierge is not all about telling my clients "Do this to avoid penalties," or "Do that to get better interest rates." I also learn many good practices from them. The successful people I have worked with, who are at the top of their industries, share many of the same habits—and I am going to share eleven of those with you today:

*Source: Wikipedia.com.

BEST PRACTICE #1:
HAVE A GOOD RELATIONSHIP WITH YOUR MONEY

The first place to start romancing your money is to develop a spending plan. You will find that sticking to a plan becomes easier over time.

BEST PRACTICE #2:
KNOW HOW MUCH MONEY YOU HAVE

You don't want your account balance to be some sort of formless, vague idea. If your spending plan is going to stick, that means getting a handle on all of your accounts.

BEST PRACTICE #3:
DON'T BLOW IT ALL ON TOYS

As great as race cars and sailboats are, they are depreciating assets. The savvy spenders I know are aware that such toys do nothing but eat away at the bottom line. So do what they do: Think it through before you make large, discretionary purchases.

BEST PRACTICE #4:
THINK POSITIVELY

In my experience, successful people have a tendency to think more positively and that makes them more productive.

BEST PRACTICE #5:
SURROUND YOURSELF WITH POSITIVE PEOPLE

You are much more likely to seal a deal or gain a referral from someone who has a forward-thinking, expansive personality as opposed to someone focused on the past. Surround yourself with positive thinkers, and the positivity will snowball.

BEST PRACTICE #6:
ASK A LOT OF QUESTIONS

The people I know who have achieved great success and wealth always ask a lot of questions—of their accountant, their financial adviser or even their mechanic.

BEST PRACTICE #7:
USE YOUR CALENDAR

Most calendars offer color-coding options to keep track of different goals or projects. They can be used by themselves or together with color-coded e-mails to pack every entry with as much information as possible. Another thing to remember is that your calendar can be used to schedule more than just business meetings. If one of your goals for the new year is to exercise more, reach for it by being more organized; use your calendar to schedule your time to work out and treat it just like any other appointment.

BEST PRACTICE #8:
DON'T GET DISTRACTED BY E-MAIL

E-mails are distracting. It's hard to concentrate on a project when being barraged by e-mails on any number of other topics. Try compartmentalizing your workflow by only checking your e-mails two or three times a day.

BEST PRACTICE #9:
MAKE USE OF SOCIAL MEDIA TOOLS

Business cards are the currency of networking. There are many different scanners on the market designed to help capture the information on business cards, yet in many cases all of that information is already available in digital format on social media sites like LinkedIn. Not only can you connect with people you've just met, you can keep current and organized with the people you've known for years. I personally enjoy seeing what connections old friends and colleagues have made and what professional milestones they've accomplished.

Additionally, LinkedIn keeps track of various networking events and mixers.

BEST PRACTICE #10:
REMEMBER THAT LIFE IS A BALANCING ACT

As important as it may be to set up a firewall between your personal and professional life, there will always be situations that don't fit squarely into the mold. Don't get discouraged by the occasional chaos that might send a shock through your organizational system. Remember your best practice…and improve it!

BEST PRACTICE #11:
LET YOUR WEEKEND BE THE END OF YOUR WEEK

Part of being organized means making time for yourself. It seems that the boundary between work and home is becoming less clearly defined as time moves on. Some things that I have found helpful in drawing the line between business and pleasure include choosing a nightly or weekly cut off for calls or e-mails from the office.

If you were to take only one of these best practices away with you, I recommend checking your bank balance every morning as a first step. From there, you can go on to make a spending plan and perfect the rest of your new financial habits—and don't hesitate to share anything new you learn with me!

CHAPTER *Sixteen*

FRAUD

*T*ax Fraud Alert: Recently reports have begun to trickle in about taxpayers receiving IRS Letter 5071C. Letter 5071C is a standard letter issued by the IRS when it needs taxpayers to confirm personal information. If you receive Letter 5071C, there will be contact information for the agency's new Identity Verification Service. There is a dedicated website and a dedicated phone number that will be provided in the IRS letter for this new department. Do not give out any information unless you have verified the authenticity of the letter. And never answer any questions over the phone.

It's no surprise that "Fraud" is the longest chapter in this book. Tax fraud and identity theft—everywhere you look, you see stories about them. It's overwhelming and scary because anybody can steal your identity; all they need is your Social Security number and date of birth, and they can file a tax return in your name.

So, how can you protect yourself against fraud?

- Never leave mail anywhere that's not secure—take it to the post office.

- Don't carry your Medicare card or Social Security card around with you.

- If you have a tax preparer, make sure they have a Personal Tax Identification Number (PTIN).

In rare instances, tax preparers have been caught siphoning their clients' refunds directly into their own bank accounts. Other thieves have been so brazen that they bragged about their crimes on Facebook. Below is a quote from one such individual:

I'm __, the queen of IRS tax fraud. I'm a millionaire, for the record.

For the record, the Queen of IRS Tax Fraud is now serving twenty-one years in federal prison.

So why does this keep happening?

The law states that the IRS must process tax returns as soon as they get them, even if your W2s and 1099s haven't been submitted yet from your employer. As a result, if someone steals your identity and files a fraudulent tax return to try to get a refund, the IRS has to process that request as soon as it receives it.

If someone files a return in your name before you do, they get the refund. If the IRS waited until April 15 to process people's returns, that would solve the issue.

I read somewhere that street crime is down because criminals are turning their attention to our tax returns. The IRS is failing, costing the federal government and taxpayers billions of dollars.

They use an antiquated system to "verify" that a return is filed by the correct taxpayer, even when they don't know for sure. Something needs to change.

****

One of my clients is actually two people: a husband and wife team who each have a physical disability. As a result, they have come to depend on home health aides to help them with their medical needs as well as everyday tasks like grocery shopping.

When we first started helping them, we didn't have online access to their credit cards, so we had to wait for the statement to be delivered every month. During the normal course of business we realized that we needed to call one of their credit card companies in order to get the most current balance. We were in for a big surprise.

In a complete reversal of the spending habits I knew my clients to have, the last six charges to one of their credit cards totaled $43,000 in purchases from Saks and Barney's. I confirmed the charges were fraudulent with my clients.

Unfortunately, I also discovered unauthorized activity in their checking account, too; there had been three phone transfers from one of their checking accounts to pay off the credit card bill!

Now I've seen credit card fraud, and I've seen people hack into checking accounts, but I had never seen someone hack into a checking account to pay the credit card bill that they fraudulently racked up. As it turns out, their goal in paying off the bill with the stolen money was to obtain a credit line increase.

The investigation into the matter is ongoing, but I personally have some suspicions about the rotating staff of aides who were in the house on a daily basis. This case was extremely unusual because of the access the criminal obtained to both the credit card and the checking account used to pay for it. It's not usually the case that a random identity thief would have access to both.

After all was said and done, my clients were able to recoup the stolen funds, but it took time and aggravation.

Shortly after that experience, I was talking to an accountant friend of mine and learned about another scam. It all started when one of his clients received a notice from the IRS telling him that he was due a refund from his tax returns. The only problem: He hadn't even filed yet.

So my friend (the CPA) contacted the IRS on behalf of his client, telling them:

- The tax returns hadn't yet been filed;
- The submitted returns were not legitimate; and
- His client was not expecting a refund in any case.

As they delved deeper into the electronic "paper" trail, it was discovered that various account numbers were off, though the Social Security number was correct, making it possible to file a bogus tax return. Luckily the IRS and the CPA were on top of it.

So from now on, whenever this taxpayer files, he has to fill out a signed affidavit with a copy of his passport and other identifying documents to prove that he is who he is claiming to be. He can't e-file for three to five years.

Unfortunately tax return fraud is something that has been happening a lot recently.

Take these statistics from the IRS:

- Tax return fraud is up 60 percent from year-ago levels.

- $5.2 billion in tax refunds were stolen between January 1 and September 21 of 2014.*

- The IRS stops nearly 5 million returns seeking refunds totaling over $20 billion.

- Each tax identity theft case takes roughly 180 days to resolve.

It's easy for criminals to e-file using a real name and Social Security number combined with a phony W-2 or fabricated Schedule C. In fact, tax return fraud is almost always perpetrated by filing electronically, with an attempt to arrange for refunds to be directly deposited into the thief's bank account. By doing their work electronically they leave behind no signed tax forms or envelopes or finger prints—and the refunds are disbursed before anyone catches on.

There is yet another way criminals can use your tax returns to make a quick buck: Unscrupulous tax preparers.

A small-yet-well-known seasonal tax-preparation firm has recently been accused of modifying the bank routing number on returns and diverting electronic refunds to their own account. Worse yet, some fly-by-night tax preparers have been caught manipulating the data on their clients' tax returns in order to claim more dependents to increase the amount of the refund they are stealing.

*From "The Tax Refund Scam," aired on Sept. 21, 2014. Steve Kroft, correspondent; Ira Rosen, producer.

HOW TO PROTECT YOURSELF

With so many high-tech scams around, my advice to people looking for new tax preparers is to ask around before you commit to a new tax professional. Verify they have strong ties to the community and that they've been in business for a while. In other words, don't go with somebody who hangs out their shingle and does tax returns only during tax season. Go with a reputable CPA firm that is open year-round.

Also: Do not respond to e-mails that say they're from the IRS. Like every other reputable vendor, the IRS does not contact taxpayers via e-mail.

Being vigilant about your privacy is a necessity in today's world, and nothing is more important to protect than your Social Security number. Unfortunately, many businesses—and the federal government—are not as careful with citizens' numbers as they should be.

While colleges and universities have ceased using students' Social Security numbers as student identification numbers, the Social Security Administration lags far behind. All Medicare enrollees receive a benefits card that is emblazoned with their Social Security number, and most of them carry it in their wallet.

People lose their wallets all the time, which is why I tell my clients and their loved ones to never carry their Medicare card, or their Social Security card, in their wallet. No one can ever get assigned another Social Security number.

Another threat is the prevalence of places asking for Social Security numbers when they have no business doing so. Just because a person or business asks for a person's Social Security number does not mean that person is required to provide it. That includes a doctor's office. Someone who finds him or herself being prompted to give up their number should be firm and confident. In the case of a doctor's office, insist that they use your insurance ID number instead.

Even at home, scam artists are angling to get access to people's Social Security numbers. The classic move is for the scammer, or phisher, to call a home and act like they know a senior—and then ask for as much personal information as they can get.

Remember:

- Medicare will never ask for someone's Social Security number – they already have it.
- Banks will never call and ask for a Social Security number – they, too, already have it.

One way to help combat this type of scam in the senior population is to keep a script by the phone so they don't get flustered or intimidated, like:

- "I'm not interested, please don't call back."
- "I'd be glad to discuss this further if I can call you back. May I have your number?"
- "Please send me something in the mail."

The bottom line is that taking basic steps to secure our own privacy is easier than it sounds. How can you organize yourself, or your loved one, to be resilient in the face of dishonest people?

FRAUD PROTECTION FOR STUDENTS

What is happening to our seniors is also happening to our young adults. College identity theft is a growing problem because college kids are easy prey.

20 percent of identity thefts are "friendly fraud"—fraud committed by people the victim knows. College students are especially at risk because of the social nature of living in dorms. It's not uncommon for students to let someone else borrow a laptop, and they rarely, if ever, create a second user account for guests.

They don't get it!

Most college students are not even concerned about identity theft. They view it as an issue that won't affect them because they don't have much money or credit. But it's really not about stealing money. Someone could use a student's driver's license to get credit card accounts, apply for jobs, loans, or any number of fraudulent activities.

Sometimes it takes as much as two years before identity fraud is discovered. To keep your identity safe on campus:

- Shred unwanted mail in a secure garbage (or recycling!) receptacle.
- Never access your bank account from a public computer.
- Establish a guest user identity for other people to use on your computer.
- Answer security questions with fictional answers.

- Never lend your ID to be used by another person.

- Install robust anti-virus and anti-malware programs.

- Never illegally download media from a file-sharing site.

- Switch to electronic bank statements instead of paper.

- Balance your checkbook. People who are unaware of their balances are at risk of incurring fraudulent charges.

College is a place where we learn about the way the world works, usually through trial and error. However, things that are as important as your identity should not be left up to chance.

FRAUD WHILE ABROAD

Imagine falling through the cracks. It's a scary feeling to find yourself in, especially if you are in a foreign country. But that's exactly what happened to my friend Jane (not her real name).

She was abroad during a recent vacation when the ramifications of identity theft reared their ugly head. Here is her story, as told in her own words:

We arrived in Paris on a Sunday, which happened to be Bastille Day. We then took a second flight to Toulouse to stay with friends in a beautiful little town nearby.

On Tuesday, we took everyone to dinner. When the check came, I offered to pick up the tab on my credit card. It was rejected after several attempts. Luckily, my husband's card worked, but I was very concerned.

Using our hosts' phone, I called the credit card company, stating to the representative that I didn't understand why this happened — I had notified the company we would be in France before we left. Her response startled me:

"You called on Saturday the 13th at 5:30 p.m., saying that you just moved to California, and in your move misplaced your card."

"But that's when we were boarding a plane, so I know it wasn't me who called you," I told her.

She said the representative recording that call had received satisfactory answers to all of the pertinent security questions: name, address, date of birth, and the last four digits of my Social Security number

The person posing as me had all my information! The representative offered to expedite the card. My imposter then asked if the rep would add someone else's name to the card, so now there are two cards: one with my name and one with this California woman's name.

The rep then told me I'd have to verify that I was who I said I was. I replied that it would be difficult for me to do so, because I was in France.

She asked how she could reach me to verify my identity, which presented a second challenge: I didn't activate the international calling plan for my cell phone before we left. Fortunately, our friends had been talking to their friends in the States via a Wi-Fi telephone service. They connected my phone to the Wi-Fi and the credit card company rep was able to call me back. Otherwise, I don't know what would have happened.

I told her to freeze the credit card. Next I had to repeat everything to the fraud division. The company ended up sending a temporary card to meet me on the next leg of our journey, which I could use for the remainder of our trip. They said a new permanent card would be waiting for me at home.

The whole episode was eerie. But the scariest part was coming home and getting calls, supposedly from the bank, asking me to verify my date of birth.

The credit card company has been extremely helpful fixing this. I was fortunate that there were no charges on the account because the thief didn't have the actual card, or the numbers on it.

I never did find out who the thief was. I called the Fraud Department to ask if they were able to catch her, but they said they couldn't release that information!

I hope that Jane's cautionary tale serves as an inspiration for you to do more to protect your identity. One thing you can do is call your bank to ask for a new set of security questions. When you are answering them this time, consider replying with fictional information. Things like your date of birth and your mother's maiden name are easy to find.

E-MAIL HACKING

In the beginning of August, one of my clients began renting a property to a new tenant. We set up a system where the rent would be deposited into a certain account at XYZ Bank, and my client proceeded to go back to her home in Europe.

Not long after this, the tenant received an e-mail, supposedly from my client. The tenant was instructed to deposit the first and last month's rent, along with the security deposit, into a bank account in Ohio. At first, I didn't understand; I didn't know my client had an account in Ohio.

And that is when I came face to face with pure evil.

After e-mailing my client to relay my conversation with the renter, I asked about the wire transfer to Ohio. "Yes, I did set this all up," the reply said. It was just a temporary measure; the rent would eventually go directly to her account at XYZ Bank, but she said she had yet to set up that account to receive deposits.

I noted that the closing salutation in the e-mail said "xs." My client usually wrote "xx."

Whenever bank accounts are involved, I don't trust e-mail as a valid means of communication. I reached out to my client over the phone and asked if she set up an account in Ohio for the first month, last month, and security deposit, and she said no. She was under the impression that we had her money, and we said no.

While we were on the phone, she happened to be sitting with the same realtor who had found the tenant for her. According to him, this sort of thing had been happening a lot to his company.

And so the puzzle pieces began to come together: the correspondence I had received from my client was actually from a hacker. After gaining access to my client's account, they had read her old e-mails enough to identify the tenant and understand the previously worked-out arrangement of depositing funds to XYZ Bank. They imitated my client's writing style and temperament—but they messed up by finishing the e-mail with "xs" instead of "xx."

As it turns out, Gmail accounts are getting hacked more frequently than others, but unlike hacking an Outlook account, the only way to get into a Gmail account is to discover the password.

There are a multitude of ways that hacking can happen:

- A key logger can be installed on your computer physically or over the web. It works by recording every single letter you type. That means a hacker has to sift through all of your personal business before honing in on your password.

- Your browser's password manager can betray you. With a few clicks in front of your computer, a hacker can uncover all of the passwords for all of the sites that it has on record. No hacking degree required.

- A packet analyzer examines all information sent to your device over a wireless network. All that is required is that the hacker be on the same Wi-Fi network as you—so beware of networks with open access and short passwords! If possible, use the personal hotspot on your phone instead (and secure that with a long password).

Given the above information, it seems clear that my client's information could have been hacked in any number of locations, both in the US and abroad.

In my business, security is our number one concern. That is the reason we change passwords every month on all client accounts. We make use of password generators that spit out the most random collection of letters, numerals, and symbols that I have ever seen. And we never, *ever* do telephone banking, banking by app, or take important instructions via e-mail.

CHAPTER *Seventeen*

ELDER ABUSE

Protecting seniors against elder financial abuse is one of my most important duties as a Financial Concierge.

Elder abuse has many faces. It might come in the form of a stranger pushing a "confidence game" where he earns the victim's trust, a caregiver charging an exorbitant rate for her services, or a family member who has a sense of entitlement to the victim's money.

To help make sure someone you love doesn't fall victim to a similar elder financial abuse scam, keep a lookout for the following warning signs:

- The appearance of a new "best friend"
- An overreaching caregiver—for example, one who opens the senior's mail

- Bank statements no longer come to the senior's address
- Unusual checks or credit card charges
- Medications go missing
- The appearance of new electronics that might be used by caregivers, such as a large flat screen television or a new laptop

You can also increase the chance of nipping abuse in the bud by recognizing what makes a senior vulnerable:

- Depression
- Being unaware of their assets
- Isolation and loneliness
- Being intimidated by technology, especially as it relates to finances
- Physical or mental handicaps that might impair his or her ability to stop financial abuse
- Having a family member with a drug or gambling addiction

It's up to us to make sure our loved ones have the support they need in order to prevent financial abuse.

As a Financial Concierge, not only do I pay bills and balance checkbooks, I also look out for the general well-being of my clients—whether that means stopping elder financial abuse or scheduling routine visits to the doctor.

WARNING SIGNS OF ELDER ABUSE

Just this week I got to the bottom of another story of financial abuse, performed in a very subtle manner. However, there were warning signs all along the way, so I thought I would share some of them with you.

The case involved a married couple who had hired me to take care of their bills and establish a spending plan, among other things. Like many people their age, they had an in-home caregiver visit them daily. She was very friendly, and it looked like she took good care of my clients, but soon a pattern started to emerge.

CLUE #1: UNUSUAL SPENDING

I visit these clients once a week to go over bills and cash flow with them. I noticed that the caregiver had a habit of walking in the room where we were meeting—and I began to suspect her of eavesdropping from another room. I didn't say anything because all I had was a gut feeling at that point.

As is the case with most retired people, my clients live on a fixed budget. In order to better manage it, we divide it into a weekly allowance and I kept a close eye on the checkbook. One day I noticed some withdrawals from the checking account that were not included in the weekly spending plan.

CLUE #2: ASKING FOR INAPPROPRIATE REIMBURSEMENT

The caregiver volunteered to take my clients' grandson to the airport and my clients gave her cash for it. I told her that I was familiar with the route to the airport and that it did not cost as much as the amount she was claiming.

Christmas time came and my clients wanted to give the caregiver a generous bonus, which is one week's salary at the end of the year. I said her contract does not allow her to accept gifts so I called the agency to discuss it with them. They approved the bonus, but something had changed in the dynamic between my client and the caregiver.

CLUE #3: DEMANDS FOR A RAISE

The caregiver developed an attitude about the money she was making. For some reason, she divulged to me that she goes into the agency every three months to demand a raise, no matter what—and that my clients have been approving every one.

THE SCAM

Through the ordinary course of my duties, I discovered that the caregiver was now a beneficiary of the husband's will ... to the tune of $50,000!

It's not uncommon for people to leave their housekeeper or caretaker something in their wills, but that is usually for a worker who has been with them for many years. This caregiver had been working for—or rather, working—my clients for less than a year.

It all came to a head while the caregiver was on vacation in Florida. I happened to run into my clients' lawyer and I asked him about this unusual $50,000 addition to their will. He acknowledged adding the caregiver, as did the husband.

When confronted by the agency, the caregiver denied any knowledge of being put in the will. All parties knew she was lying. While she was still in Florida, my clients terminated their relationship with her, and she never came back to their house.

A STUDY IN SCAMMING

Elder abuse is one of the cruelest crimes, but there are warning signs you can look out for. In the following case, the warning signs shared one thing in common: a new best friend.

Here's how it happened:

- In California, a woman entered into an online relationship with a gentleman from Brooklyn. She gradually emptied her savings account for this individual, fully expecting to be paid back.

- Meanwhile in Eastern Europe, some hackers got hold of my client's routing and account numbers and used them to manufacture fake checks, which were then bundled up and sent to Brooklyn.

- The man from Brooklyn told the woman from California that a "friend" of his owed him some money. His scheme involved telling her that his friend would be sending reimbursement on his behalf – when in fact, the checks were stolen from my client's account.

- The woman from California was told not to worry about who the checks came from. She then deposited the checks, they cleared, and she spent all the money. Later she was told that the checks were "self help," and that she was on the hook for all the money she spent.

- When my client and I went to the police to file a report, we were told that nothing could be done locally. The matter was turned over to the bank's international fraud department. According to them, this was the work of a global fraud ring, which made it nearly impossible to trace.

It turned out that the woman from California was just one of an ensemble of players—some of whom were not even aware of each other's efforts—devoted to parting this gentleman from his money. It was a drama staged across twelve time zones.

TALKING TO ELDERS ABOUT ABUSE

I am lucky to be in a profession where my skills can be used to directly help seniors. Our parents have survived a lot, in addition to raising us. Just as kids are eager to prove their independence from their parents, elderly parents want to prove their independence from their adult children. More often than not, though, things like paying bills in a timely manner get forgotten, and soon utilities start to get cut off. That's usually what spurs us into looking into home care or assisted living facilities.

But how do we get them to think about assisted living? One of the ways to get a senior thinking about moving is by talking to them about the family heirlooms.

From personal experience, I know that a large part of the anxiety someone feels when leaving their house behind comes from a sense of being "in charge" of all the mementos. When my daughter and I helped my mother clean out her house, we packed a station wagon full of pictures and memorabilia to take home with us. My mother said she felt a huge sense of relief knowing that they were being kept in the family.

Other things that you can do to help broach the subject:

- Pick a time and place without distractions to bring up your concerns
- Use "I" statements and speak only for yourself
- Consider having a mutually trusted person present, or even a mediator
- Keep it slow and talk about one issue at a time
- Keep your own emotions and reactions in check
- Don't bring up the past
- Listen

The consequences of saying nothing and doing nothing can be tragic—from missed doses of important medications, to major back injuries.

I recently heard of a case where a woman was alone and immobilized, out of the reach of her phone and her emergency alert device. For days she laid there, until a neighbor called the fire department. Her door was broken down, and she was taken to the hospital.

That case could have turned out so much worse.

Stories like these are what keep adult children up at night, but they can also serve as motivation for us. It's never too early to start taking baby steps today with your favorite senior. Going through the old photos together is a great way to start—you may find that Mom or Dad can still teach you a thing or two.

CHAPTER *Eighteen*

SURVIVING THE HOLIDAYS

The holidays are a great time of year to show appreciation for the people you are thankful to have in your life.

There are a variety of ways to show how thankful you are, from handmade gifts to cash—but also remember that words of gratitude can go a long way. But what exactly should you give, and to whom?

Here's a list to help you choose your gifts wisely:

- **Au Pair, Live-In Nanny, or Home Health Aide:** Up to one week's pay and a gift from your child(ren), if gift-giving is not against agency policy.

- **Regular Babysitter:** Up to one evening's pay and a small gift from your child(ren).

- **Day Care Provider:** A gift from you or $25-$70 for each staff member who works with your child(ren) and a small gift from your child(ren).

- **Live-In Help:** One week's pay as a cash tip.

- **Housekeeper/Cleaner:** Up to the amount of one week's pay and/or a small gift.

- **Barber or Beauty Salon Staff:** Up to the cost of one salon visit divided for each staff member who works with you.

- **Personal Trainer:** Up to the cost of one session or a gift.

- **Massage Therapist:** Up to the cost of one session or a gift.

- **Pet Groomer or Dog Walker:** Up to the cost of one session or a gift.

- **Pool Cleaner:** Up to the cost of one cleaning to be split among the crew.

- **Garage Attendants**: $25-$100

- **Newspaper Delivery Person:** $10-30 or a small gift.

- **UPS or FedEx Delivery Person:** Small gift in the $20 range. Most delivery companies discourage or prohibit cash gifts.

- **Superintendent:** $25-100 or a gift, depending how friendly and helpful your super has been.

- **Handyman:** $15-40, depending how much you use their services.

- **Trash/Recycling Collectors:** $10-30 each, if private. Some regulations may prohibit collectors from accepting gifts.

- **Yard/Garden Worker:** $20-$50. If they work often, give up to a week's pay.

- **Mail Carrier:** Mail carriers working for the United States Postal Service are only allowed to accept the following items during the holiday season:
    - Snacks and beverages or perishable gifts that are not part of a meal.
    - Small gifts (travel mugs, hand warmers, etc) that are clearly no more than $20 in value.
    - Perishable items (large fruit baskets/cookie tins) must be shared with entire branch.

    Mail carriers may not accept cash gifts, checks, gift cards, or any other form of currency.

AND FINALLY, REMEMBER ...

Any gift or tip should always be accompanied by a short, handwritten note of appreciation. Words of gratitude go a long way!

AFTERWORD

MY WISH FOR YOU

Your house may seem small when viewed from Google's satellites, but to you it is the most important thing in the world. Its walls protect your family and your beloved pets through four seasons. But like anything else worth loving, it requires constant attention—and that ain't cheap!

I hope that I've answered some of your questions about being the CFO of the most important organization in your life. If I've done my job, you've learned from the successes and failures of my friends, family members, and clients—and now, you don't have to learn the hard way.

I wasn't always as financially organized as I am today, and that is why I've shared these stories. The tips I've shared in this book come from my heart, and I hope that they will find a place to dwell in yours. My wish for you is to become empowered and self-sufficient, confident and self-assured, and to think outside the box when confronted with life's ups and downs.

We are lucky to live in an age when there are so many outlets to share our experience-based wisdom, and I hope one day to read your ideas on one of them. Until then, stay in touch, and keep doing what you're doing!

ACKNOWLEDGMENTS

Thank you to the many people who saw me through this book.

First, thank you to my editor, Dan Ruisi, inspired me to come up with these great ideas, and tirelessly helped me format this book for publication.

I would also like to express my gratitude to my designer and editor Bryna René Haynes, who flawlessly created a beautiful interior and cover design that I am proud to see come to fruition.

I would like to thank my clients for all of their valuable life lessons that gave me an abundance of knowledge and experience.

This book would be a lot thinner without my anonymous colleagues who supported me by participating in my polls. Their unique stories and life lessons have already helped people.

I want to thank my team member Sharon Wilson for her unending office support that allowed me to spend the time writing this book.

I want to thank my coach and mentor Fabienne Fredrickson, who motivated me to write this book, and without whom I might not have done so.

None of the success I enjoy today could have happened without the influence of my parents, Sylvia and Sidney Heft. They taught me at a young age that hard work never hurt anyone. My mother's independence as an entrepreneur in 1955 showed me the impact a woman could make with life experience as her only guide.

And last but not least, I want to thank my daughters, Sarah Mizrahi and Willa Goldfeder, who inspire me every day and are living proof that women can indeed have it all.

ABOUT *the* AUTHOR

Judy Heft is a personal CFO, life advocate, and wellspring of financial wisdom—whether you are a busy parent, young person struggling with student loans, or a high-net-worth philanthropist.

Judy's early career began in her parents' retail clothing store. As the store's buyer and bookkeeper, she became familiar with bill-paying, accounts receivable, balancing the company checkbook, and maintaining good relationships with vendors and customers.

After leaving the family business, Judy was contacted by a friend regarding the financial situation of his mother. She was elderly, and completely dependent on others to care for her. Judy quickly saw the cast of players that surrounded her new client were draining her vitality and her checking account. For the first time, Judy realized the scope, far reach, and often intangible nature of elder financial abuse.

The skills Judy brings to each client are on tap for any situation. In the twenty years since Judith Heft & Associates was founded, Judy has seen it all; from less-than-honorable people insinuating themselves into the wills of older Americans, to resolving identity theft—and educating her clients on how to avoid it again in the future.

Learn more about Judy and her programs at www.judithheft.com.

Made in the USA
Columbia, SC
04 March 2018